Ex-Prisoner Possibilities With Real Estate Investors

Rehabilitating Properties & Lives

Rev. Mike Wanner

Copyright Rev. Mike Wanner, October 4, 2017

Selected Images Used by License

Table Of Contents

Table Of Contents 3
Introduction 4
1 - Why I am Writing This Book 5
2 - Disclaimer 6
3 - What is a Real Estate Investor 7
4 - The Needs Of a Released Prisoner 8
5 - Ex-Prisoners Need To Market Themselves 9
6 - You May Be Nicer Than the Tenants 10
7 - Doubling Your Efficiency 11
8 - Things That You Can Offer a Real Estate Investor 12
9 - Things That Your Real Estate Investor Can Offer You 13
10 - Advance Letter Plan 14
11 - Advance Letter 15
12 - Listing of Skills 16
13 - Detailing Of Skills 17
14 - Freemium Model 18
15 - Think of Serving Others 20
16 - Can You Help Carry A Message 21
17 - Can You Help Community Service 22
18 - Can You Help Communication 23
19 - Thank You 24
20 - Don't Worry Ever 25
21 - Resource List 26
22 - Angels Please Prayers 28
23 - Private Channeling 29
24 - Reverend Mike Wanner 30

Introduction

I invite every reader to consider ideas that can create freedom for taxpayers from the extreme costs of imprisoning vast numbers of our fellow citizens. We have taken for granted that we somehow can afford these expenses.

Alas and unfortunately, the costs of incarceration are about to eat up the quality of the American Dream. We are all gradually being banished to involuntary servitude to our insecurities.

Yes, we are threatened by great evil in the world. There is no need for us to overreact. There is some justification for the restrictions that are imposed upon those who have been convicted of a crime.

As taxpayers, we in the greater community have an interest in how our tax dollars are spent. Incarceration is a considerable expense, and if there were unlimited funds in our national budgets, there would be no need to consider changing anything unless fairness was a prominent goal.

Unfortunately, national budgets around the world are stretched by government expenditures, and it may make sense for us to evaluate the reasonableness of our expenses. We could find there are little opportunities for prudence.

We could also find that there are options not yet considered. This book is an invitation to look at some new ideas.

1 - Why I am Writing This Book

I hope that this book continues the work started by my other books and continues to enhance the lives of Prison Employees, Prisoners, Taxpayers and the Families of Each of these groups.

The title shift in this book indicates that getting started is the priority. Real Estate like prisons is very complicated, and after publishing more than thirty books on prisons, it became clear to me that there is an opportunity in connecting them.

Both Prisons and Real Estate have risks and I wish everyone to know up front that they need to do their own "Due Diligence" to evaluate the risks and the opportunities and go forward only when they are confident in their ability to handle the risks, live up to the responsibilities they take on and prepare to be flexible enough to succeed.

Nothing that I suggest will absolve you of your responsibility to run your own life and be responsible for all your decisions. Sharing some wisdom here is not personal advice as you will have to engage your own creativity and hire professionals when you need them.

2 - Disclaimer

I, the author, am not involved with prisons or prisoners but am sharing what is coming to me in an effort to spread understanding and trigger conversation that can be helpful. It may be that the discussion needs finessing and I invite your wisdom in the mix.

Nothing in this book is a personal life recommendation and should not be relied on for the critical decisions that you can make as you reclaim your freedom.

Opportunity may be found within this idea, but risk can also be found so please be diligent and precise with every step you take toward your freedom. Please Choose well and use a lot of discernment. Protect yourself from frustration and prepare to be selective and to discriminate so that everything you choose meets both your immediate and long-term needs.

3 - What is a Real Estate Investor

A real estate investor is a person who focuses on opportunities to do any of the following - buy, rehabilitate, upgrade, modify, change the use of, refinance, rent, lease, joint venture or rezone property so as to modify the value of the property.

Investors are independent business persons who may specialize in one or more aspects of the real estate business. Their independence may offer ex-prisoners many opportunities that could not be available from traditional employers.

Independent investors may focus on many different opportunities, and many of them move from one project to the next. Some of the projects may be prestigious where they only want the best people with the best credentials working on their properties.

The same real estate investor with prestigious properties may also have low-end properties where cost is a significant determinant after a minimum standard is met. Herein may lie value for a potential ex-prisoner employee.

An ex-prisoner who can find a reasonable independent real estate investor can get many of their needs met.

4 - The Needs Of a Released Prisoner

A released prisoner has basic needs:

1. A Place to Live
2. Food
3. An Income
4. Transportation
5. Connectivity to something or someone

Investors can be negotiated with if they feel that a released prisoner can offer them the value that they cannot get elsewhere at the same price.

5 - Ex-Prisoners Need To Market Themselves

Please do not let the chapter title above scare you off because that is not the intention. It is essential that you increase your appeal to a potential independent real estate investor by answering unasked questions so that assumptions are not made that have you appear less desirable than you actually are.

I will list below some things from my dialogue series that I suggested might be in a prisoner profile if an agency was trying to market a client to a foreign nation.

Prisoner profile formats could vary from bureau to bureau, but they could include:
1. Credit Report
2. Educational Report
3. Criminal Record
4. Skills and Certifications
5. Family History and obligations.
6. Children and spouses
7. Prisoner performance during incarceration
8. Any Violence History or lack of one.
9. A prisoner declaration of intention, goals and readiness.
10. Prisoner motivation.

Once you consider your specifics, then you need to shift in to reframe mode so that you have an honest and revealing Profile. It should list and highlight all your strengths and allow minuses be honestly reported and little noticed.

6 - You May Be Nicer Than the Tenants

Real Estate investors do not always have the nicest clientele so many of the things that you might be self-conscious about at a major corporation could be a non-issue when it comes to an independent investor.

I encourage you to set aside whatever you think of yourself when you talk to a real estate investor. The universe of their ordinary experience may well be the average citizen of the city wherein you want to reestablish your life.

The goal is to listen well and focus on what they tell you are the requirements of the job are then you can wind up in a satisfactory situation.

The most important part of your search will be your persistence to find the right opportunity. It may not be easy, but neither are other valuable accomplishments.

Thinking outside the box with a view of the big picture could be the key to your success.

7 - Doubling Your Efficiency

Part of the reason that I encourage you to consider Investors is that they can offer you a double value for your effort and you can offer them an extra benefit for hiring you.

They are in the housing business. You need housing. A match made in heaven when mixed correctly.

Security for some Investors is an issue, and it would not be a bad idea for you to propose to live in their places under renovation to provide an additional level of security while you are staying there.

Because you may need to call the police, they should be encouraged to provide you with a cell phone, so you can do that.

The right investor could provide you housing, communication and a modest income that can keep you going until opportunity knocks louder. You might also find that the investor niche fits you well for employment and an enterprise opportunity.

8 - Things That You Can Offer a Real Estate Investor

Real Estate investors are not really very accustomed to having people look after them so why don't you be the exception and look at everything like it was yours and be totally loyal all the time.

Things to investigate and report without being asked:
1 Property values in an area
2. Rental Prices in an area
3. Schools in an area
4. Transportation Options in the area.
5. Church affiliations in the area
6. Childcare resources in the area
7. Food stores in the area
8. Shopping Center options in the area
9. Non-Profit Resources
10. Athletic Fields
11. Census information that shows well
12. A list of your recommendation s for their consideration.

9 - Things That Your Real Estate Investor Can Offer You

Real Estate investors who rely on you could make significant efforts to your success. When you are totally loyal all the time, you might get unexpected benefits.

Some things you might get:

1. A living Space at Little to no cost.
2. A reasonable enough stipend or income to stay out of jail.
3. An Advocate
4. Use of a Cell Phone
5. Consistency
6. A human connection to eliminate the isolation which does in so many.
7. A friend
8. A steady enough gig.

10 - Advance Letter Plan

A reasonable time before your discharge, communication can be initiated to sort through investors and look for potential candidate hosts. Depending on your ability or the ability of family and friends to communicate, your options could vary significantly.

Patience and persistence will be needed so do not get dismayed if it takes a while or seems fruitless. You can only succeed if you persist long enough.

If there is access to a computer, research into the public image of the potential investor/employer can allow you to customize an offer that will have much more appeal.

11 - Advance Letter

Dear Mr./Mrs _____:

I (or _____) will be looking for work after _____.

I have (or s/he has) outlined skills below and attached a listing of all available competencies and would appreciate being added to your help wanted e-mail notice list.

I have also included the story of my past life, the purposed project for my life going forward and my motivations.

Pease reach me via ___Phone or ___E-mail or ___Letter addressed to _____
at_____.
Or call _____at _____.

Respectfully (A subtle but powerful declaration of respect)

_____
_____
_____

12 - Listing of Skills

The goal is to get a job. Any real possibility will work as long as it gets you focused and motivated and a foot in the door.

Real estate investors will need building maintenance skills frequently so it will be helpful for you to develop some competencies in work skills that they will need. The basics are:
    Plumbing
    Electrical
    Painting
    Cement Work
    Customer Service

While many investors are sophisticated business people, there are also a lot of one-man or one-woman enterprises who can benefit from personal assistant type services.

All business skills could be included in your skill list:
    Computer Skills
    Accounting
    Bookkeeping
    Public Relations
    Advertising
    Hiring
    Project Management
    Decisiveness

13 - Detailing Of Skills

When you look at a product in a store, you want to know all that the product can do for you after you purchase it. You may want to read the description and all the specifics of what is in the package.

In this effort, you are the product, and you know all the capabilities, and you may not want to share too much too quickly because you know that can trigger the rejection that you do not need. It could be a big mistake to hold back.

Know that if you do not put out ALL YOUR SKILLS, you will not likely be hired. It is not a time to be bashful

14 - Freemium Model

Have you ever noticed the adds about a free report or book or premium that is offered free in exchange for your e-mail address or mailing address. These advertisements are trading something tangible to get your attention to a topic that they wish to promote.

This is perfectly legal and proper, and it is a technique that you can consider to promote yourself. The obvious question may be - What can I offer?

You can offer your time in support of something that is needed by the receiver. Now I know that you might say that you will not work for free and I understand that position. I volunteer a lot and gets lots of satisfaction for doing it.

A lot of young people volunteer in public service projects to learn about a service or industry. It is not unusual for Volunteer effort to evolve into a career.

Candy strippers at hospitals can evolve into workers, technicians, housekeepers, nurses, and doctors. Human interaction can bring great rewards.

Never doing anything for anybody can evolve into a life of loneliness and isolation. I would think that ex-prisoners may have had enough of that to last them a lifetime.

Choices are always yours, and I do not have a complete list of all the options that are available to you. Only you know what tickles your fancy and there can be many things in life that keep you going when times are hard.

I like the idea that Giving and Receiving are one and the same. There is a reciprocity to life in that the good that you put out can be like a boomerang and come back to you in the same or a very different way.

It is unlikely that other folks will care about your needs unless you first care about theirs.

For your life to be renewed, you need to consider changing the way that you look at everything and then you can change yourself.

15 - Think of Serving Others

If

You

Focus

On

Serving

Others,

That

Can

Serve

You

16 - Can You Help Carry A Message

Be A Messenger of Better Options

Things You Can Do

1. Develop patience, understanding, and plant seeds to a crop of possibilities.

2. Study the laws and ask questions.

3. Google Prison Reform Topics on the internet and read up on all the efforts out there and support those that you agree with.

4. Help the legal representatives of the people to understand what works and what does not.

5. Be respectful of the efforts of others.

6. Read about the struggles of the Correctional Authorities and advise options that you can see but they cannot.

7. Help the families of those who are incarcerated.

8. Look out for and support the children of those who are in prison.

17 - Can You Help Community Service

Be A Community Service Angel
Things You Can Share To Improve Quality of Life

1. Teach Parents not to buy Toy Guns that can get their child killed by mistake. Toy Guns Are Obsolete.

2. Help Addicts have a Prayer, and a chance at http://AngelRaphaelSpeaks.com/Prayers/ Click on Drop down menu and choose.

3. Help Alcoholics have a Prayer and a chance at http://AngelRaphaelSpeaks.com/Prayers/ Click on Drop down menu and choose.

4. Help People Prepare for Health Care Emergencies http://angelraphaelspeaks.com/non-eng-med-hist/

5. Help Non-English SpeakersCommunicate & Save Lives with http://angelraphaelspeaks.com/non-eng-med-hist/

6. Help Bring Peace to Troubled people by sending them to http://Create-A-Prayer.com

7. Help Reduce Stress at http://StressReleaseCoach.com

8. Help prisoners and their families find some peace at http://AngelRaphaelSpeaks.com/Prisons/

18 - Can You Help Communication Read and Advise Skills Needed

Things You Can Do Pro Bono

1. If you read any of my messages and you have an opinion, I would love to hear it.

2. If you read any of my messages and you have a clarification, I would love to hear it.

3. If you read any of my messages and you have an idea, I would love to hear it.

4. If you read any of my messages and you have an objection, I would love to hear it.

5. If you read any of my messages and you have a comment, I would love to hear it.

6. If you read any of my messages and you have a variation, I would love to hear it.

7. If you read any of my messages and you have any of the above, I would love for you to write about it elsewhere also.

Volunteer Editors Welcome

Volunteer Beta Readers Welcome

19 - Thank You

For Considering These Ideas

20 - Don't Worry Ever

It Does Not Help Prayer Still Does!

Resource: http://www.Create-A-Prayer.com

21 - Resource List

Distant Healing Sessions (or Join Mail List) – Write To mikewann@voicenet.com

Books by Rev. Mike at **www.Amazon.com**

Veterans Healing Six Pack
1. *Trauma Healing Options for VA Hospitals: Help for Veterans to Own Their Healing and their future.*
2. *Trauma Healing Action Steps for Veterans: Help to Start Healing*
3. *Trauma Healing Action Steps for Veterans: Empowerment*
4. *Trauma Healing Action Steps for Veterans: Forgiveness*
5. *Trauma Healing Action Steps for Veterans: Thought Freedom*
6. *Tea For Veterans: Welcome One Home*

PTSD Power Pack:
1. *The PTSD Project: Turn Pain To Power*
2. *PTSD & Soul Retrieval: Putting One Back Together*
3. *PTSD & The Purple PAD: Calling all Scientists and PTSD Patients*

Angel Raphael Speaks Volume 1: Take Courage! God Has Healing in Store for You!
Angel Raphael Speaks Volume 2: Take Courage! God Has Healing in Store for You!
Angel Raphael Speaks Volume 3: Take Courage! God Has Healing in Store for You!
Angel Raphael Speaks Volume 4: Angels, Addicts, Alcoholics & Prisoners – Oh Yeah!
Angel Raphael Speaks Volume 5: Prisoners Caring for Alcoholics - Australia In Miniature Projects Intro
Angel Raphael Speaks Volume 6: Prisoners Caring for Addicts - Australia In Miniature For Addicts
Reiki Journaling from Japan
Reiki Is Alive: God's Great Gift
Four Parts to Healing
Distant Healing: We Are All Connected
Stress Release Energy Work: How To Cope

Does Reiki Love Heal Cancer?
Group Consciousness
Salute To Philadelphia VA Medical Center: Thank You
Reiki Transcript for Reiki 2 & 3 Channels: Dr. Usui Is That You?
God Bless Kindle & Amazon
Puppies Are Different From People
If Your Dog Dies
Toy Guns Are Obsolete
Great Spirit Made Children With Red Skin: AND
The Cage of Fear: Is Not Locked
God Made Children Red, Yellow, Brown, Black & White: Greet Each Child With Kindness
Emergency Medical Kindness In The Cradle Of Liberty: Big City – Cracked Bell
Angels Are Always Around Addicts and Addicts: Help Is Near Now! Invite It In!
Angels Are Always Around Addicts and Alcoholics: Volume 2 - Tools To Help Re-Light Your Life
Prison Jobs Now: Providing Care For Addicts And Addicts
Controlled Care Communities Concept

Little Books at Kindle.com by Rev. Mike:
English Medical History Questionnaire For Non-English Speakers
English Language Helper For Non-English Speakers
Wise Wonderful Women Are The Well Of The Family
Answers for Test & Research: Dowsing Power
Crisis? Reiki! Baby? Reiki!
Bible References For Healing
Angel Raphael Speaks – Prisons
Angel Raphael Speaks – Veterans
The Saint Off Interstate 95

Angel Raphael Speaks through Rev. Mike Wanner. Please visit
http://www.AngelRaphaelSpeaks.com

22 - Angels Please Prayers

Addict's
Angels of Healing Selected
Help Me to Stay Directed
Come To Me From The Sky
I Am Ready to Succeed Not Try
If I Don't Invite You In
I Might Not Win
I Have Been Lost For Too Long
Help Me To Stay Strong

&

Alcoholic's
Angels of Healing On High
Help Me to Stay Dry
Come To Me From The Sky
I Am Ready to Succeed Not Try
If I Don't Invite You In
I Might Not Win
I Have Been Lost For Too Long
Help Me To Stay Strong

From

http://AngelRaphaelSpeaks.com/AAAAAAA/

23 - Private Channeling

Angel Raphael Speaks a series of free messages that are channeled through Reverend Mike Wanner for the Highest good and Highest Healing of all concerned.

Many questions arise about Reverend Mike doing private channeling, and he does help with that so e-mail him.

Reverend Mike is available worldwide as a psychic channel, emotional release facilitator, spiritual energy practitioner & teacher, and public speaker. He looks forward to meeting you soon!

Email - mikewann@voicenet.com   215-342-1270

PRIVATE SPIRITUAL READINGS/channelings or Spiritual Healing Sessions: Telephone or in person. Rev. Mike is available for private, one-on-one intuitive sessions with you, his Guide Family, and your Guides. He helps by offering clarity on emotional situations about your life, your purpose, your spirituality, and the release of stuffed emotions and cellular memory.

Connect to the love of your Guides today!
Contact Rev. Mike for an appointment.

Sessions available:

Spiritual Readings
Angel Channeling
Distant Reiki Healing
Distant Clearing of Stuffed Emotions
Distant Clearing Cellular Memory
Distant Clearing Energy Blockages
Distant Clearing of the Chakras
Customized needs
Mastermind dowsing responses to yes/no direction finding questions.

Rev. Mike is a facilitator of healing. He brings you and the Divine together so that you can align with the Divine and have a great time and a great life. All healing is between you and God, as it should be. Go ahead and start without Rev. Mike. Visit his prayer site http://www.Create-A-Prayer.com. Take the first step NOW.

24 - Reverend Mike Wanner

Rev. Mike Wanner started his metaphysical and ministerial studies with Reiki in 1993 and had studied seven styles of Reiki in the U.S., Japan, Canada, Denmark and Australia. He is certified to teach. He became certified to teach Integrated Energy Therapy in 1999 and co-taught the first IET class of the new Millennium. Mike began dowsing in 2001.

Ordained as a Metaphysical Minister of the International Metaphysical Ministry and an Interfaith Minister of the Circle of Miracles Ministry, Rev. Mike practices and teaches spiritual energy therapies in the Philadelphia Area.

Rev. Mike holds ministerial degrees from the University of Metaphysics and the University of Sedona. He is a Pastoral Care Associate of Aria - Frankford Hospital. He taught at the National Academy of Massage Therapy and Health Sciences.

Rev. Mike was a faculty member of the Medical Mission Sister's Center for Human Integration's School of Integrated Body/Mind Therapies in Fox Chase, Philadelphia, PA for twelve years.

Rev. Mike is licensed by the teaching of Intuitional Metaphysics to practice Spiritual Healing and Scientific Prayer. Mike is also a Prayer therapist.

Rev. Mike was elected in 2007 to the status of "Fellow of the American Institute of Stress."

In 2008, Rev. Mike became a practitioner of Coincidental Recognition as he incorporated the CoRe system into his spiritual healing practice.

In 2009, Rev. Mike trademarked a new healing process called Quantum Quatro! Subtle Energy System Support®.
In 2011, Rev. Mike joined the outreach program known as the Health Advantage Group.

In 2012, Rev. Mike became a Certified Professional Coach by The Master Coaching Academy and Joined The Personal Empowerment Group.

Prior to his Metaphysical, ministerial and coaching studies, Rev. Mike worked for Sears Roebuck and Co. while in High School and after graduation, until he joined the U. S. Air Force in 1965. He returned to Sears from Vietnam in 1969 and stayed until 1978. His final Sears assignment was as an efficiency expert in Methods - Operational Research and Development.

He volunteered with Burholme Emergency Medical Services from 1969 and is still a Life Member and Board of Directors Member. He started a private ambulance company in 1975 and worked professionally in the field until 2001 when he devoted his full attention to real estate investing, healing, coaching, and writing.

www.ingramcontent.com/pod-product-compliance
Lightning Source LLC
Chambersburg PA
CBHW050036230526
45470CB00003B/1311